Everyone has a brain. Ou

how to move

how to talk

how to play

and how to smile

I sometimes have to go to the hospital for a check up.

At the hospital, the doctor showed me a picture of the brain inside my head!

My brain has a bit missing,

this is called the **corpus callosum**

The corpus callosum is like a bridge

It takes messages from one side of your brain

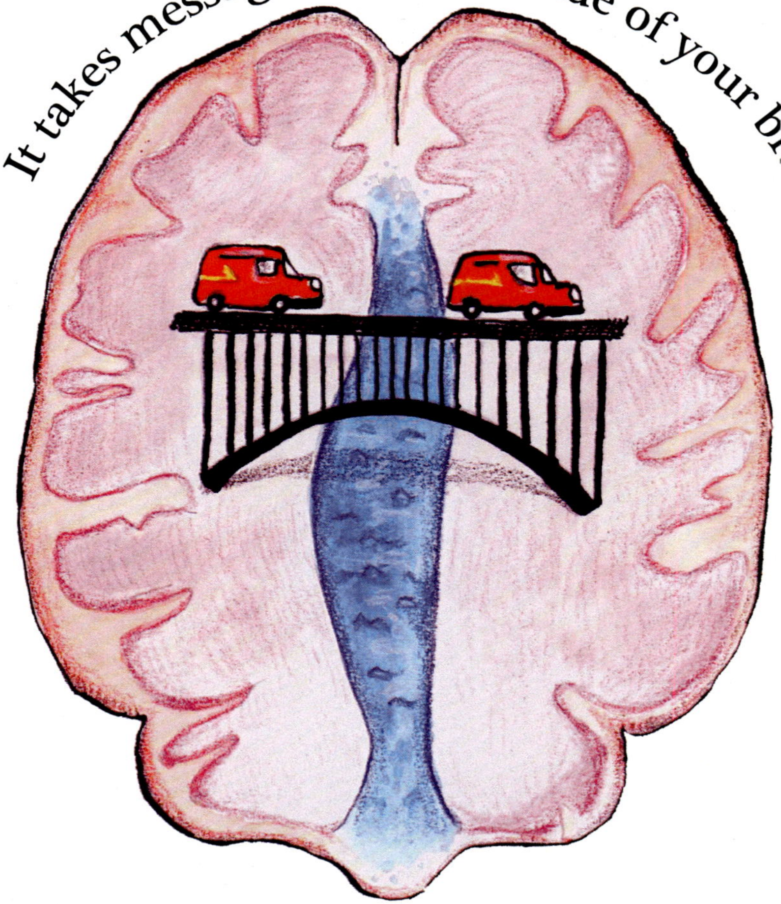

to another

Because I don't have this bridge, the messages have to find another way round which sometimes takes a little longer and I find some things a bit difficult.

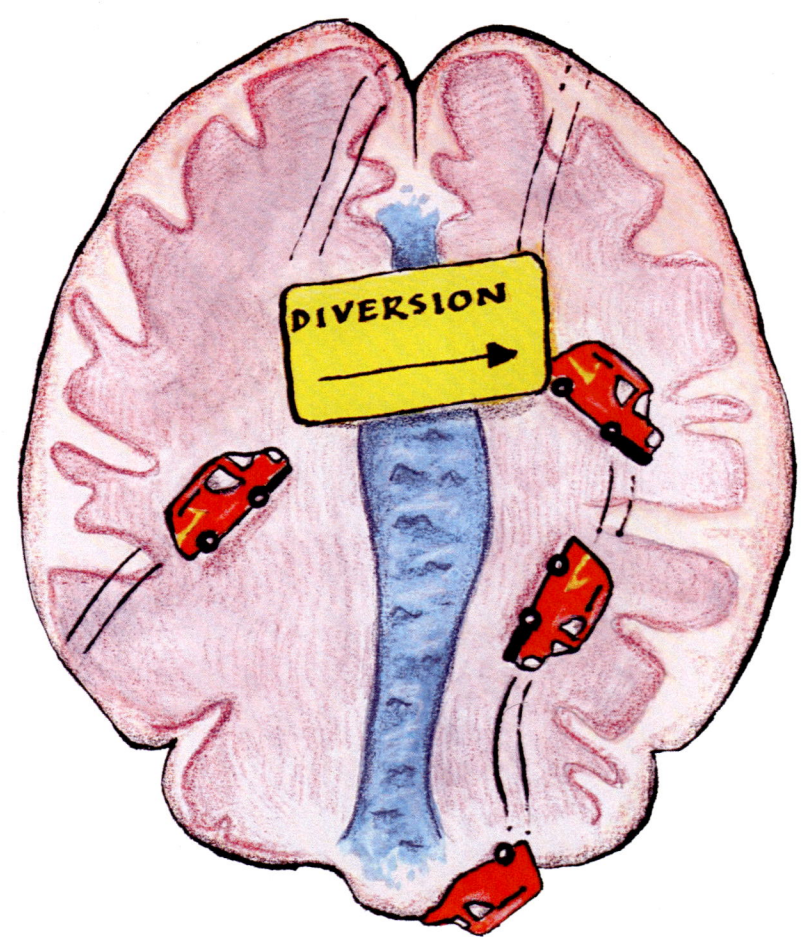

The doctors call this **agenesis of the corpus callosum**. This is also called **ACC** which is handy as that is easier to say!

some are short

ir, brown hair, red hair, blonde hair...

I wonder what it would be like to have

We like different things and we are all able to do different things.

Some people with ACC might find it difficult to walk

or catch a ball.

Other people with ACC might have trouble learning how to talk.

Sometimes I find it hard to understand what other people mean and how they feel.

I might stand a bit close

and I have to remind myself that some people like more space.

I can get help to learn new things

and I always feel really proud of myself when I do.